Poems for a stormy night©

To Frazer,
Good luck and I hope you like it,
The drummerman
23/8/13

G Merrifield

Poems for a stormy night©

By Terrence Merrifield

Copyright notice

Text and Artwork Copyright 2013 @ Terrence Merrifield

Terrence Merrifield reserves the moral right to be identified with his work.

978-1-291-52054-5

Poems for a stormy night©

By Terrence Merrifield

Contents

Copyright notice..2

MIRROR MIRROR..7

SAD JOY..9

WAITING FOR YOU...11

DECAY..13

WORLD...14

PASSING ON...15

SHADOW..17

GREY..19

GRAVE..22

FORGOTTEN...24

INSIDE..26

AETERNALIS (eternal)...29

REICH TRAVELLER..31

ARCAN..34

Poems for a stormy night©

By Terrence Merrifield

SPIRIT...37

STONE...39

FADE...41

GONE...43

NIGHT WALK...46

Incident in a wood..52

Lacrimosa...54

THE LIGHT...56

TO NOTHING...58

Poems for a stormy night©

By Terrence Merrifield

PHANTOM

Down the road

Walking

Through the wood

Walking

Across the field

Walking

Along the beach

Walking.

Onward without purpose or

Direction

Road and field, beach and wood

Poems for a stormy night©

By Terrence Merrifield

No recollection.

Never tired, ever walking

Phantom never still

Till the future is

No more, then

Phantom can be free.

Poems for a stormy night©

By Terrence Merrifield

MIRROR MIRROR

The face was so, familiar,

Yet somehow different.

It was, how you say?

All used up, each line

Etched so deep that they

Screamed of pain endured,

Of suffering so personal

That the story can never

Be told.

Eyes blank in defensive emptyness

As if too much has been witnessed

Poems for a stormy night©

By Terrence Merrifield

Too much absorbed.

The face, so familiar, turned

The nerves cold with fear and loathing

Until, unable to endure anymore

Turned away from its own reflection.

SAD JOY

You make me sad

With joy, an

Optimistic pessimism

I soar to bright uplands

And down to the very

Depths of disenchantment

The love i have for you

Is a passion of extremes

A destablisation of emotion

Yet i cannot be without you

For you are my very heart

Existence and life

Poems for a stormy night©

By Terrence Merrifield

I never knew i was capable

Of such surrender, such devotion

You truly are my

Angel of the morning.

WAITING FOR YOU

When the spring rain

Waters our little piece

Of heaven, and

The warmth of

The early morning

Sun awakens the

Song of our love

Remember that i

Will always watch

Over you, even till

The world passes

Away.

Poems for a stormy night©

By Terrence Merrifield

Forever have i loved

You, forever will

I love you.

Till then adieu

I will be waiting

Waiting till we

Are united and

Become one.

DECAY

A dwelling place

Of broken dreams

Rags of non restistance

A pallid, insipid

Loss of will,

Collections of abandoned

Futures

Bloody irredeemable

Bruised pain of

Dispair

Life without

Necrosis!

WORLD

By the light of

A single candle

And the coming

Of the spirit

The breath of

God descends upon

A fractured world

Pieta il mondo.

PASSING ON

Released from the past,

Moving on.

Farewell, farewell

Old compatriot

Perhaps, in some

Other place or time

We will meet again.

Behind, the road

Narrows, ahead

Widens.

What adventures new

Lay in the future?

Poems for a stormy night©

By Terrence Merrifield

What dreams will be

Fulfilled, or confounded?

Into that mist of

Imminent expectation,

Striding onward into

A new dawn.

SHADOW

Death did not

Change me.

Life used me up

And cast me aside.

Now i am just a

Shadow of was.

I cannot see you

Clearly, for the

Dead see the

Living only as

Images of the past,

And the shadow that

Poems for a stormy night©

By Terrence Merrifield

Walked beside me

Then, was just

Myself, as i

Became, shadow following shadow.

GREY

Autumn thrilled

As cold fingers of

Grey mist rose

Wraith like from the

Forest floor.

Brown and russet

Leaves scattered

In a cacophony of

Rustling sounds

As darkness descended.

Will-o-the-wisps

Poems for a stormy night©

By Terrence Merrifield

Danced fast and

Silent amongst the

Silhouetted trees.

The moon cast

Her baleful light

Upon the risen mist,

Mixing silver moonbeams

With its grey,

Leprous, clinging dampness.

All was still, as

The forest waited

For the coming of

Poems for a stormy night©

By Terrence Merrifield

The dawn, the

Renewal of

Waking movements.

GRAVE

There was no

Fear, when

Ghost

Gathered at

Twilight in

The yard of

Graves.

Burned by their

Sadness, i felt

Their longing

For life.

Drifting in line

Poems for a stormy night©

By Terrence Merrifield

they formed a

Silent procession.

Emanating emotions

Of pity,

I tried

To convey

This message,

Love never dies.

FORGOTTEN

You speak of

Freedom and

Liberty,

But where is

Mine?

Housebound i

Live in

Isolation,

Waiting to

Die,perhaps!

Yet i want

To live!, to

Poems for a stormy night©

By Terrence Merrifield

Contribute to

The world.

So much to

Give, so much

To love, yet

I struggle in

A void of an

Unbeing.

An atmosphere

Of soundless

Sight, a

Disappearing

Nobody.

INSIDE

Between the rolling

Of black planets

And the

Empty spaces.

The vibration of

The song of

Spheres

Filter down into

The mind.

Their song,

On cosmic

Wind, echo

Poems for a stormy night©

By Terrence Merrifield

Through the

Universe.

A whispering of

Timeless ages.

Of the past,

Confronting the

Present, and

Looking for the

Future.

The mind sings the

Song of the spheres,

Until disintegration

Poems for a stormy night©

By Terrence Merrifield

Free it to join

With the

Universal mind.

AETERNALIS (eternal)

I saw the

Light of the

World,

Walking as a

Man!

I called,

"Lord, Lord,

In your mercy

Pity me".

The word came

To me. as a

Breath, and

Peace,

Embraced me.

The incendium Amoris (fire of love)

Enraptured me,

Purified me,

And i saw the

Light of the

World,

As a halo.

Scitote quoniam(know ye that the)

Dominus ipse est (Lord, He is)

Deus (God)

REICH TRAVELLER

He didn,t care

When none

spoke.

He didn,t care

When none noticed

Him.

All that mattered

Was the road.

That long silent

Road.

It issued from

Nowhere, and

Went, nowhere.

Screams and cries

Around him, were

Nothing to him.

The road.

Only mattered.

Straight it was,

Mist shrouded and

Dark.

Eternal was the

Journey, through

Life, through

Death, through.

Poems for a stormy night©

By Terrence Merrifield

The the

Endless seasons

Onward, ever onward.

Existing in

Non existence, a

Dream, nebulous

And insubstantial

A void, that

Was a,

Something of

nothingness.

Yet he was!

ARCAN

" I,m not impressed, not impressed at all, where,s the prey, i,m starving". So began the desperate search for food, as Arcan crawled slowly through the undergrowth. The wood had never seemed so hostile, so devoid of pity. Arcan knew that if he did not get nourishment soon, then nothing would matter ever again! Water was no problem. It was the life giving nourishment that he so desperately needed. Energy must be conserved, or he would not have the strength to catch the prey. He waited, quietly and expectantly, yet with the growing concern, that, come the hours of darkness, he would have to protect himself from the, whispering death! Not that only, but he knew others, like himself, we also starving, and who would not hesitate to finish him off, kill him, perhaps even eat him. Starvation can drive anyone into unspeakable acts of evil. Survival is always the bottom line.

Arcan watch with growing apprehension as the Suns light grew fainter. Selecting a spot by a large fallen branch, his faceted eyes searched the surrounding area, alert always for rivals, and of course , prey! His strength was fading. He could feel the weakness in his limbs, yet, through determined will power, forced his mind of his empty stomach. The wood grew

Poems for a stormy night©

By Terrence Merrifield

increasingly darker as he fought the desperation entering his thoughts. Then, he thought he saw a movement, ever so slight, yet only a yard or so away, to his left. Stareing hard at the spot, he carefully, slowly inched closer. Inch by inch, stopping every few seconds, to ensure he was not detected the prey came into view. It was a large one! He hoped that his energy and reflexes we enough to catch the tasty looking creature. Speed was his advantage. With a single swift stabbing motion he could be feeding in just a few precious moments. Moonlight now gave the whole area a silvery light, and the shadows hid him, or a least he hoped they did! Closer and closer he came, until he could feel the disturbed ether as his prey moved about. Then he had a clear run! It was now or never, life or death. His concentration was total. Then he realised that his prey was about to fly away. Gathering all his pent up energy, he charged. With a leap of total recklessness he caught the creature in his deadly embrace, and with practised ease stabbed into the thorax of his prey. Now the struggle for life really began, as the creature twist and turned, rolled and pushed, fighting desperately for its life. Arcan hung on grimly, till, after what seemed an eternity, the creatures struggles became weaker, until he felt the last, the death throws of his prey. He fed. Hardly stopping to to look to his own safety. Then, as the beams of the Moon became obscured by dark clouds,a rustle of sound alerted him. It came

Poems for a stormy night©

By Terrence Merrifield

from directly above him. He knew, instinctively what the sound was. The flapping of huge wings! Looking up he could just make out the form of a bird. A large, nocturnal bird, an Owl! He froze, knowing that he could not make it to safety, if the Owl decided to attack. With fear he saw the bird look at him with its huge eyes. But, just as he had given up all hope, the Owl turned away from him, and with a powerful flap of its wings, it flew into the night. Seconds later he was hiding under a fallen tree, safe. Yet he knew safety was relative. His world, the hunters world, was never really without peril. Today he had fed, and would live, but tomorrow was an unexplored country. Spiders, like himself, he knew, were never truly out of danger. He preyed on some, others preyed on him! He would rest, till the coming daylight, when the struggle for survival would begin all over again!

SPIRIT

Spirit walks the

Avenue of silent

Dream, an

Ectoplasmic being

Wailing in a

Place of non

Existence.

Black planets in

A black universe.

Spirit knows

Eternity, and

Walks the path

Of thoughts.

Here he was,

Here he will be,

Here he never was!

Spirit talks to

Dream,

An echo of

Presence, a

Trace of,

Something,

Intangible.

Mist in the mind!

STONE

It is cold.

Night surrounds me

As a brooding presence.

Trees whisper

To each other

In the wind.

Serene, the

Moon glows in

Her remoteness.

Incapable of movement

I stand rigid.

A dark silhouette

Poems for a stormy night©

By Terrence Merrifield

Washed by the breath

Of timeless ghosts.

Hauntingly eternal,

A perpetual presence,

Monolith!

FADE

Lamentations of

Isolation

Cri de Coeur

Silence.

Woe unto the

Dispossed,

Pity to the

Forgotten.

Pain of separation,

The ghost of

Poems for a stormy night©

By Terrence Merrifield

Unfulfilled promise.

Distant echo of

Regret,

Dull vibration of

Unrequited passions.

An ocean of

Interior pain.

A fading from

Existence, a

Journeying into oblivion!

GONE

Gone,

Just, gone.

Here, then not.

A space

Created by

Absence.

A void of

Something, alien.

"They were here

Iknow they were!

For i remember them,

But now

Poems for a stormy night©

By Terrence Merrifield

Nothing!"

Isolations of

Loneliness.

Adrift on a

Sea of silence.

Where are you?

In the Earth, or

In the Air, or

Just in

Imagination?

I searched for you,

Poems for a stormy night©

By Terrence Merrifield

In the streets,

In the fields,

In the deserted

Places.

But you are

Gone,

Just Gone,

Nullibiety!

NIGHT WALK

The night,

Dark, stormy,

And rain pouring down.

Is that just the

Pitter patter

Of the rain?

Or is there someone

Or something,

Following?

The gray street

Echoing to footfalls,as

Poems for a stormy night©

By Terrence Merrifield

A lone figure walks

Into the darkness of night.

Eyes, alert with fear,

Searching the stygian blackness.

Is that a shadow of a man?

Or just a shadow, cast by

The light of a liquid moon?

Onward,

Moving,

Listening.

Is that footsteps?

Or just, imagination?

Poems for a stormy night©

By Terrence Merrifield

The hard rain continues to

Fall noisily on the cobbled road.

The sound is;

Yes, like

Someone following!

Stop, turn,

Search the dark road.

Is anyone there?

Is that a movement,

Just there, by the wall,

In the shadow?

Can,t see, rain too hard.

Walk faster.

Poems for a stormy night©

By Terrence Merrifield

It cannot be far now.

The lights of the city centre

In view, yet still

Some distance,

But not, too long

To reach their

Comforting glow!

Not long, not long,

Keep moving, keep

Speed up!

Just around the next corner,

Then safety!

Police constable Tony Stubbs,

Poems for a stormy night©

By Terrence Merrifield

Cursed his luck to

Have foot patrol on

A night like this!

A scream!

Was it human?

proberly not,

Too faint to be near,

Maybe an Owl,

Or, some such night bird.

Still must not tarry,

Duty to perform,

Roll on break time!

Poems for a stormy night©

By Terrence Merrifield

At fortyseven

High street,

A shabbily dressed woman,

Waits in expectation

For her lover, in

The mean bedsit

She calls home.

She waits in vain!

He never comes,

And he never will!

Incident in a wood

Blood on a leaf.

Cobweb on a branch.

Movement,

The spider makes no noise.

Victim.

A silent thrust,

Death.

the web quivers and

Shines in

The moonlight

The Owls eye

Poems for a stormy night©

By Terrence Merrifield

Pierces the dark.

A silent witness!

Life goes on.

Unconcerned,

The Owl goes

In search of nourishment.

Lacrimosa

When winter comes

And the cold

Pierces my heart,

My wings will not

Bear me aloft.

I will not endure, for

My enemies are many

And my defences feeble.

I wait for the dark.

I shall not see the

morning frost

White upon the

Ground.

I will perish

Silently,

And the down of

My feathers will

Blend with cold earth.

Perhaps, the heat of

A weak Sun

Will bring a

Single drop

Of morning

Dew, to be a

Tear,

Just for me.

THE LIGHT

Silver is the colour of night.

Its lustre shines in the darkness

And lights the way.

Gold is the colour of day.

It destroys the darkness.

Mankind lives in the silver.

Man cannot live in the light,

for it burns him to nothingness!

Silver is the light of man,

for man lives only in reflected light.

Gold is the unreachable light.

Gold is the eternal light,

Poems for a stormy night©

By Terrence Merrifield

The aura of perfection.

None can face the gold without destruction!

God resides in the light.

Only the pure can see into the light.

Beware! seek only the silver,

For only through reflected light,

Can man see perfection.

TO NOTHING

Through a mist

I walk

The Zodiac line,

Amongst the sacred

Signs twelve,

Unaltered by time.

I drift and

I dwell

Among the stars

So bright, so

Alight, with

Shining, changing hues.

Poems for a stormy night©

By Terrence Merrifield

The globe of

My birth

Is fading from

View, as i

Too am

Fading, slowly away.

I feel no

Pity or

Pain, nor will

I live again

Upon the Earth!

I am dead!

And who?

Will remember me?

Poems for a stormy night©

By Terrence Merrifield

Who will remember

me?, o

I am nothing!

Poems for a stormy night©

By Terrence Merrifield

Poems for a stormy night©

By Terrence Merrifield

978-1-291-52054-5